The Phoenix Living Poets

A
ROUND OF APPLAUSE

by

NORMAN MacCAIG

CHATTO AND WINDUS

THE HOGARTH PRESS

1962

Published by
Chatto and Windus Ltd
with The Hogarth Press Ltd
42 William IV Street
London WC2

*

Clarke, Irwin and Co Ltd
Toronto

Contents

Contents

Memory Two Ways

Along a road, all corners,
Into whose deepest secret
The huge Atlantic pokes
One of its crooked fingers,

Through tunnels damp with rowans,
Past Loch an Ordain, winking
With islands in its eye,
One of my selves is going

Ten years ago. Ten summers
Have quenched their flowery bonfire,
Ten winters have flamed white,
And there he is, dark figure,

A fact for time to curse at,
Sending on to my envy
A sky green as an egg
And two capsizing ravens

And moist ferns in a gully
And the sound of slapstick water
Perpetually falling downstairs.
If he could see his fellow,

His ten years older brother,
How many roads, all corners,
He'd have to look along
To find him here, dark figure

In enviable landscapes
Where space is all of meanings
And clownish times fall down
To beautiful Atlantics

Whose presence, breathing inland,
Enriches all it breathes on
With trembling atmospheres,
With sounds becoming soundless.

Sound of the Sea on a Still Evening

It comes through quietness, softly crumbling in
Till it becomes the quietness; and we know
The wind to be will reach us from Loch Roe.
From the receding South it will begin
To stir, to whisper; and by morning all
The sea will lounge North, sloping by Clachtoll.

Gentlest of prophecies. The most tottering grass
Stands still as a stiff thorn, as though its root
Groped not in sand but in sand's absolute
And was itself disqualified to pass
Into a shaking world where it must be
Not grass but grasses waving like the sea.

Three heifers slouch by, trailing down the road
A hundred yards of milky breath – they rip
The grasses sideways. Waterdrops still drip
From the turned tap and tinily explode
On their flat stone. An unseen bird goes by,
Its little feathers hushing the whole sky.

And yet a word is spoken. When the light
Gives back its redness to the Point of Stoer
And sets off cocks like squibs, pebbles will roar
At their harsh labour, grinding shells to white
And glittering beaches, and tall waves will run
Fawning on rocks and barking in the sun.

Rain on Fence Wire

What little violences shake
The raindrop till it turns from apple
To stretched-out pear, then drops and takes
Its whirling rainbows to the ground?

Once, I remember, you, too, fell,
Quenched, to the world, and in your vanished
Face I could see no call for help
Nor news of what had brought you down.

Was it the world itself that quaked
Enormously beyond my knowing?
Or tiny claws, that perch and shake
From yards away a rainbow down?

No difference . . . I look and see
The dry wings flirt, the small ounce soaring
And with its leap a shower of drops
Flames down, released into the grass.

Translations of Innocence

Small girls on bibles sailed away
Through pinks and whites and curly clouds
And boys hung through a black Nor'easter,
Gallant upon the rattling shrouds.

They used to. But the heavenly shores
Are empty round the sea of glass
And oilwells gush on tropic islands
Gunboats scarcely dare to pass.

Yet restless in their present tense,
The little siblings, scarcely born,
Jostle around the same old places,
The gates of ivory and horn.

And paradisal images
Of pride and babies, blood and fear,
Obscure with trailing fumes of glory
The dreadful fact of being here.

And each one gulps his apple down
Under the dark forbidden tree.
Who would be angel now and notice
What's mirrored in the crystal sea?

Failed Mystic

A stone remarked what he'd no answer to
And trees showered secrets he could only share
In remote reaches of himself – a country
He seldom travelled to. When winds were fair

He coasted with them, smelling of the Spring;
When they blew contrary he downed his head
And bullocked on, an ugly opposition,
Swearing to find himself – and found instead

What a wind is. He could not bear to be
The odd man out, the man out, or the man;
He grudged the grass the grass, he envied water
And coveted meaning's meaning. He would scan

Himself for monsters, or for dew. His mind
Leaked over being, trying to soak in
And by assumption to extend his empire
Beyond the confines of his rotting skin

To the remotest reaches of a stone
As though to look from there and see a place
That he could love, that he could, somehow, envy,
Although it had an only human face.

Crocus

Affiliations make no meaning to
The crocus single in the unheeded world
Nor, one would think, the force of being blue –

More than the world reflects upon itself
And with expertise hoists blue petals up.
Complacence is my way of feeling safe

Who make paternal, lover's, cousin's kin
Of all the world, something that a blue
Crocus can bear to find enlargement in,

As though a principle, pecked by sparrows, was
Sprung from a bulb and that bulb was the sun
And it a principle and I their cause

And fatherly, loverly, cousinly, by incest
Becoming all my creatures, survey them all
And, for the moment, think the crocus best.

Choices

Hold in white plaster what a turn would be
If turns would end, as they would never do;
Or with a brush prevent a red from reddening:
Words do this, trafficking between me and you.

Or you forestall the world from being it.
It stays, as though it cannot breed away
Into its selves, frozen in four seasons.
You stage it so; I watch you in the play.

And yet your will, like my words', is for reds
To redden round themselves till they are one
Immediate spectrum, where worlds would deliver
One simple season, and all changes done.

And you and I, engrossing what we are,
Would have one word to say, no time to lose.
We know this when we stop the turn from turning
And make old history the end of news.

The bird last night, whiskered with moths, flew out
From more than yonder into more than there –
But not for us: a bird flew, only, leaving
A sketch of flight behind it in the air.

One bird, and comic, in one place that we
Have chosen into existence – steep down they fall
To be a mode of us, where we together
Tell time to stop, who listens not at all.

Spraying Sheep

Old tufts of wool lie on the grass.
The clipping's over. But once again
The small quicksilver flock come pouring
Down from the hill towards the pen.

Dogs coax them to the roofless steading.
They bunch, plunge forward, one by one.
When half's outside and half within, they
Make a white hourglass in the sun.

The dogs run on the ruined walls,
Swinging their tongues, their minds all sheep.
The zinc bath winks, the stirrup pump
Guzzles the primrose one foot deep.

Then out they come, bounding high over
Nothing at all, and ramble on
The shining grass – not quicksilver
But golden fleeces, every one.

Lighthouse

Gorgon in greed, but not effect, it glares
A thing to life and back again.
A hill jumps forward, then it isn't there.
A tree explodes in tree shape. Flashes devour
This house's natural death – it has more than twenty
Punctual resurrections every hour.
Bad Christians think that one is more than plenty.

Bad disbelievers, too, are troubled by
Their disbelief – how weak it is;
And in the dark look for that whirling eye
Whose maniacal rigidity might swing
Them into high relief . . . The sea, too busy
Inventing its own forms, bucks by, leaving
The mind to spin, the dark brain to grow dizzy.

Culag Pier

A moderate jargon – winches, cries in Gaelic,
Cordage against the sky: most moderate when
A gull slews in with icefloes in his eyes
And a seal of crimson dapper on his beak;
A frosty distance follows where he flies.

Yet see him, pick-and-run, as he hauls a herring
Through slats of a fishbox, ululating oaths
In a sort of Eskimo at whatever stands
Between his greed and his belly – see him swerving
Out of infinity, steered by guts and glands.

The moderate jargon takes the two things in –
The winged etcetera in his etcetera wastes
Or small town gangster pillaging a slum –
And, puffing incense of brine and oily iron,
Jubilates briskly of its kingdom come.

The moderation is, of course, no mask.
Grace is hilarity; and this scene has
Good nature, in two meanings, as its meaning,
Where a transcendence feeds on guts and makes
No bones of it, nor thinks it worth the screening.

And the observing mind, in its own sun,
Takes it as so. Bright baskets swing between
The darkness and the light and herrings go
Where they could not have guessed in their broad ocean,
And ropes seem tangled, but they are not so.

Always First Morning

And spaces, with no sound at all
Assembling like a threatening crowd,
Contracted into selves – a wall
Between each cloud that touched a cloud.

On mountain tops, round ptarmigan
Grunted from burrows in the air
And with a flash of red began
Plumply to whirr to here from there.

Salmon deduced themselves from what
Became a brown froth over stones.
They winked and sidled into thought,
Wavering their long monotones.

And hayfields gently lurched. And slopes
Were buckled with red cattle. Tracks
Tangled green parishes with ropes
And laid tall fields upon their backs.

Larks climbed the air, more cliff than tree,
Each improvising shelf on shelf.
A roof, discovering how to be
Ran helter-skelter through itself.

Horizons prowled. How could they pounce
Out of the cage that distance is
To tear rose bush and water flounce
Or fawn on homely presences? –

Like that small curdling of the air
That played with two white stones and smiled
To see a sparkling Everywhere
Perched on the knuckles of a child.

And everything unfolded till
A naked Eden gathered round
The tree that on a distant hill
Laid its crossed shadow on the ground.

Other Self

My inmost creature, Caliban perhaps,
Perhaps St Francis (at least, a sort of dunce)
Sits, like a Chinese sage listening to
A colloquy of summer afternoons,
Inscrutable understanding on his brow.

The panegyric that his silence is
Comes clear to me (that other sort of dunce),
Written with smallest wrinkles, the stillness of
A sleeve, the half-beginnings of a glance,
An air of sensuous contemplative.

What pool rocks what white petal in his gaze?
What fluffed out bird is blobbed upon its bough?
I can see mountains, but they are not his
Tressed with cascades and single in the sky,
Removed by poems from glittering paddy fields.

If I could make the epigram he is,
The seventeen syllables saying exactly what
They exactly do not say, this other man
Would see such blossoms frosting with their light
The barbarous province he is banished in.

All Being Equal

A black wave bangs on timber
And slavers past. We go
Bouncing by lucky shores.
The sky sways overhead
Where blue stars spurt and crumble.
The sea turns in its bed.

All that is in this narrow
Abridgment of what is
Bulks big and equal. Thin
Spatters of water are
No less themselves nor nearer
Than cliffhead or than star.

As though skies could remember
And winds be filled with all
That winds are, no line falls
As treacherous boundary
Beyond which myth and monster
Are told, are as they say.

You make it so. You, sitting
Dark in the sternsheets, break
Webs of perspective. Space
Hauls all its treasures in
And time, with plots for plotting,
Has no time to begin.

The moon climbs up, converging
With miracles. It shows
How running waves can go
Against but cannot halt
Our rakish island, forging
Past bays as white as salt.

And the black wave bangs on timber
And hoists you up against
The sky and not its mask,
The rock and not its stone
In time and not its minutes,
Where nothing is alone.

Ordinary Homecoming

All that had been before had led to this
Hand in the air, about to knock. It was
The funnel tip from which events fanned back,
Through which they'd pour, and with no filtering gauze.

The night had measured out miles that were long
Under the Plough – but not to be shortened by
The looking all ways mind, balanced between
Its once upon a time, its by-and-by.

Not one shade could be grudged, one oily glint
From the black sea. All that had been before
Must be in the narrow moment, that held it all,
When the clenched fist knocked lightly on the door.

Chair scraped, steps sounded. Light shot violently
Across the grass and quenched the shaking Plough.
The purse upon the doorstep gave a jump,
Turning to toad. A bouncing dog said How.

And resolutions filled the lighted room.
Click went the wireless, off. And words were said
That in an hour would lay a future down
Beside a past, safe in one narrow bed.

Choir and Solo

The choir she trod from, clumping up the nave,
Gave her an element for soaring in,
Not a mere ladder, not a climbing stave.

It had no colour, though it called for one,
Nor shape (though, vaguely, what about the sea?).
Its sort of weight rejected pound or ton.

It simply took the place of what had been
A chiaroscuro and a smell of dust
And an uprush of stones, with space between.

Having no gravity, it had no height
And no extension, since it went nowhere:
A small ubiquity, like day or night.

At any rate she soared in it and made
By singleness a measure and a height
Nothing to do with dust or light and shade.

A low roof could have kept it in, a sky
Not have contained it. When she was up there
The music had a death for living by.

For its extensions took a dying shape
And moved towards its end. They made themselves
A law whose judgments they could not escape.

And when she stopped, ubiquity again
Eased the stones back, and in its formal space
The dust danced down from the rich windowpane.

In a Level Light

Sheep wander haloed, birds at their plainsong shed
Pure benedictions on water's painted glass.
The gentle worm rears up her hooded head
And weaves hot sermons under her steeple of grass.
Saints objurgate from thickets, angels bank
Over the sea: and its crisp texts unfold,
Silvering the sand's ecclesiastic gold.

Accepted in it all, one of its moods,
The human mind sits in its sense of sin,
Hacking a cross from gross beatitudes,
The price to pay warm in its purse of skin,
And sees out in that bliss, and out of its,
An angel tilt, dive into texts and float,
Working his god down his rebelling throat.

Good Neighbour

As buzzard riding a crinkle in the air
Hangs on his muscles and gathers in two eyes
The whole economy of parishes;
His mind does so, and tilts to keep just there.

Iconoclasts going crooked in the dark
Cast their shrewd cloaks about them: as he folds
The light he is transparent in and yields
His own blurred image, for its shattered sake.

Over a rock the sea sighs, hoisting up
Its helpless weight on to the dry land;
As he laboriously makes himself a tide
And over alien elements starts to creep.

The untroubled paradigms think nothing of
Such tiny triumphs; into his lungs they breathe
The final careless seasons of their breath
He takes as hate, but might, no less, be love.

In reaches that he carries in himself
They stretch past his imagining; and he
Trembles towards a lost identity
That they forever have been keeping safe.

Midnight, Lochinver

Wine-coloured, Homer said, wine-dark . . .
The seaweed on the stony beach,
Flushed darker with that wine, was kilts
And beasts and carpets . . . A startled heron
Tucked in its cloud two yellow stilts.

And eiderducks were five, no, two –
No, six. A lounging fishbox raised
Its broad nose to the moon. With groans
And shouts the steep burn drowned itself;
And sighs were soft among the stones.

All quiet, all dark: excepting where
A cone of light stood on the pier
And in the circle of its scope
A hot winch huffed and puffed and gnashed
Its iron fangs and swallowed rope.

The nursing tide moved gently in.
Familiar archipelagoes
Heard her advancing, heard her speak
Things clear, though hard to understand
Whether in Gaelic or in Greek.

Things in Each Other

To fake green strokes in water, light fidgets,
A niggling fidget, and the green is there,
Born of a blue and marrying into blue
With clouds blushed pink on it from the upper air.

And water breathing upwards from itself
Sketches an island with blurred pencillings,
A phase of space, a melting out of space:
Mind does this, too, with the pure shapes of things.

Or the mind fidgets and a thought, grown green,
Born of nowhere and marrying nowhere,
Fakes a creation, that is one and goes
Into the world and makes its difference there.

A thing to be regarded: whose pure shape
Blurs in the quality of the noticing mind
And is blushed pink and makes the hard jump from
Created to creator, like human kind.

The Shore Road

The sea pursued
Its beastlike amours, rolling in its sweat
And beautiful under the moon; and a leaf was
A lively architecture in the light.

The space between
Was full, to splitting point, of presences
So oilily adjustable a walking man
Pushed through and trailed behind no turbulence.

The walking man
With octaves in his guts was a quartertone
In octaves of octaves that climbed up and down
Beyond his hearing, to back parts of the moon.

As though things were
Perpetual chronologies of themselves,
He sounded his small history, to make complete
The interval of leaf and rutting waves.

Or so he thought,
And heard his hard shoes scrunching in the grit,
Smelt salt and iodine in the wind and knew
The door was near, the supper, the small lamplight.

High up on Suilven

Gulfs of blue air, two lochs like spectacles,
A frog (this height) and Harris in the sky –
There are more reasons for hills
Than being steep and reaching only high.

Meeting the cliff face, the American wind
Stands up on end: chute going the wrong way.
Nine ravens play with it and
Go up and down its lift half the long day.

Reasons for them? the hill's one ... A web like this
Has a thread that goes beyond the possible;
The old spider outside space
Runs down it – and where's raven? Or where's hill?

Preacher

The cloud he speaks from has another voice
That, needing no words, minces none and splits
No doubtful hairs with stropped and shining wits.

Its thirdly fourthly and its brethren are
All one to it, and it makes nothing of
Division and distraction, hate and love.

He pounds his metaphysics, and its dust
Joins all the rest, waltzing above the pews
Where chosen people wonder what they choose.

The infiltration of an angel would
Gloze the proceedings; but his fiery face
Would burn like brimstone this defenceless place.

And what pedantic lunacy could bear
The logic of a presence? – Or could raise
Blind eyes to that mild and catastrophic gaze?

The crow voice caws. The mind saws up and down
And thinks to follow the first Word and Will
By trying to divide the Indivisible.

The other voice speaks things into the air,
Its own disguises, utterances that fall
As kirk and congregation, angel and all.

One word pronounced all ways – hard text to read,
That spells out heaven and pronounces hell
And rings a steeple when it builds a bell.

And the congregation (that disguise), led out
From sorts of Egypts, singing as they go,
Cross more and wider Jordans than they know.

Familiar

Perhaps there is a colour that could be
Grand ancestor of colours, or a shape
Whose idling into space must vanish as
The million shapes there are. Perhaps one could,
By feeling thought, know what it is to be.

The midday stands, the morning falls away.
No clearer than the wheatfield in its wheat
Or water circling its enormous spaces
The question folds around itself and makes
Morning fall upright, midday stand away.

And on a circle made of centres, all
Jugglings and glosses and hard aptitudes
Eat their rapacious selves. Round moons come down
In heavy clarity on what seems a mountain.
Another clarity shows them, is them all.

Through their transparencies perhaps one could,
By thinking feeling, idle into what
Is the true opaque, progenitor who mocks
Us with our decadences and whom we
Pursue with love, would fly from if we could.

Moorings

In a salt ring of moonlight
The dinghy nods at nothing.
It paws the bright water
And scatters its own shadow
In a false net of light.

A ruined chain lies reptile,
Tied to the ground by grasses.
Two oars, wet with sweet water
Filched from the air, are slanted
From a wrecked lobster creel.

The cork that can't be travels –
Nose of a dog otter.
It's piped at, screamed at, sworn at
By elegant oyster catcher
On furious red legs.

With a sort of idle swaying
The tide breathes in. Harsh seaweed
Uncrackles to its kissing;
The skin of the water glistens;
Rich fat swims on the brine.

And all night in his stable
The dinghy paws bright water,
Restless steeplechaser
Longing to clear the hurdles
That ring the Point of Stoer.

Snow in Princes Street

Slush on the ground. Taxis
Go slurring by. The railing
Holds up its snowy wicks –
Beyond, the castle sails.

Pale on the dirty clouds,
High in the air, not climbing,
A second moon announces
A second sort of time.

The night shrugs distance off,
But it won't go. It whispers
Of wastes, migrations, gulfs
And swarming memories.

Nothing's enough. Horizons
Surge out from the weak lamppost.
Their rings spread, rushing towards
Shores that no waters lap:

Whose secret has this centre,
Where brown snow sobs in gutters
And every minute opens
What never will be shut;

Where light, crippled on pavements,
Takes its long journey backwards
To the fiery sun, the vast
Source of the white, the black;

And where caves glow for Aladdins –
No Sesame to open
But coins that children jingle,
That taste just like the snow.

Fine to be them. But lonely
To be the tall man staring
At tinsel sprawling down
On snowfield and shambling bear

And on that globe of crimson –
Cottage where crooked women
Keep strange children for ransom;
As he in his red room

Keeps what was once his childhood.
Who will redeem it? A moment,
Only, may go by riding
And toss him his purse of gold.

What more than a moment matters –
Small wizard, whose small whisper
Lays the tall champion flat
And makes songs sing in earnest?

The high clock there, glum angel
Whose self is his own halo,
Measures off Edens; clangs
On each its sullen gate.

– Yet still a tree of gardens
And snowy windows, rooted
Deep in a dark field,
Holds up its dangerous fruit.

And a strange will in its branches
Twinkles its scales. It hisses
Like wheels in the watery slush.
It coils in these dark minds.

And inklings grope in spaces
And breathe up from dark cellars
And lie like newspapers
Scuffed round the drinking well;

Where a drunk man, blunt lips pouting,
Sucking a thumb of water,
Is joined by a silver string
To nightblack watersheds.

Poachers, Early Morning

The net was spread upon the ground.
As though a sort of cloud it lay
Where fish had failed to fly. They cleaned
Their choking cloud, their Milky Way
Whose constellations bulged in sacks
Soon to be heaved upon their backs.

Enlarged in the enlarging light,
Two bustling primitives, they shook
A sixty yards long diagram out;
Four huge deft hands reached out and took
Precisely knots of weed and wrack,
The smooth, the varicose, the black.

Centuries, generations made
A natural ritual of a crime
And with their less than human hand
Lifted two rascals out of time
Till, each his own ancestor, they
Carried their holy spoils away.

Byre

The thatched roof rings like heaven where mice
Squeak small hosannahs all night long,
Scratching its golden pavements, skirting
The gutter's crystal river-song.

Wild kittens in the world below
Glare with one flaming eye through cracks,
Spurt in the straw, are tawny brooches
Splayed on the chests of drunken sacks.

The dimness becomes darkness as
Vast presences come mincing in,
Swagbellied Aphrodites, swinging
A silver slaver from each chin.

And all is milky, secret, female.
Angels are hushed and plain straws shine.
And kittens miaow in circles, stalking
With tail and hindleg one straight line.

Still Life

Three apples, if they are apples, and a jug,
A lemon (certain), grapes, a fish's tail,
A melting fruitdish and a randy table:
Squared off from other existences they struggle
Into a peace, a balancing of such power
As past and future use in being Now.

Still life, they call it – like a bursting bomb
That keeps on bursting, one burst, on and on:
A new existence, continually being born,
Emerging out of white into the sombre
Garishness of the spectrum, refusing the easy,
Clenching its strength on nothing but how to be.

Nice lesson for a narrative or for
A thing made emblem – that martyrs in their fire,
Christs on their crosses, fêtes and massacres,
When purified of their small history,
Cannot surpass, no matter how they struggle,
Three apples (more than likely) and a jug.

Water Tap

There was this hayfield,
You remember, pale gold
If it weren't hazed
With a million clover heads.

A rope of water
Frayed down – the bucket
Hoisted up a plate
Of flashing light.

The thin road screwed
Into hills; all ended
Journeys were somewhere,
But far, far.

You laughed, by the fence;
And everything that was
Hoisting water
Suddenly spilled over.

Mutual Life

A wildcat, furfire in a bracken bush,
Twitches his club-tail, rounds his amber eyes
At rockabye rabbits humped on the world. The air
Crackles about him. His world is a rabbit's size.

And in milky pearls, in a liquefaction of green,
One of ten thousand, spattering squabs of light,
A mackerel shuttles the hanging waterwebs,
Muscling through tons, slipping them left and right.

What do you know, mind, of that speck in air,
The high insanitary raven that pecks his claws
A thousand feet up and volplanes on his back
And greets his ancient sweetheart with coarse caws?

You tell a hand to rise and you think it yours.
It makes a shape (you have none) in a space
It gives perspective to. You sink in it
And disappear there, foundered without trace.

And dreadful alienations bring you down
Into a proper loneliness. You cry
For limits that make a wildcat possible
And laws that tumble ravens in the sky.

– Till clenched hand opens, drowning into you,
Where mackerel, wildcat, raven never fall
Out of their proper spaces; and you are
Perpetual resurrection of them all.

Loch Sionascaig

Hard to remember how the water went
Shaking the light,
Until it shook like peas in a riddling plate.

Or how the islands snored into the wind,
Or seemed to, round
Stiff, plunging headlands that they never cleared.

Or how a trout hung high its drizzling bow
For a count of three –
Heraldic figure on a shield of spray.

Yet clear the footprint in the puddled sand
That slowly filled
And rounded out and smoothed and disappeared.

Outsider

I watch the lush moon fatly smirking down –
Where she might go, to skirt that smouldering cloud,
Is space enough to lose your image in.

Or, turn my head, between those islands run
Sandpapering currents that would scrub the dull
Picture away in suds and slaverings.

Even this grass, glowered at with force enough,
And listened to with lusting, would usurp,
In its beanstalk way, the walking, talking thing.

I choose it should not go. I turn from these
Paltering beautiful things, in case I see
Your image fade and myself fade with it –

A dissipation into actual light:
A dissolution in pure wave: a demise
In growth of a good greenness, sappy and thick –

And think myself a foreigner in this scene,
The odd shape cramped on stone, the unbeastlike, clear
Of law and logos, with choices to commit . . .

Thump goes the wave then crisscross gabbles back –
As I do now till, wave to wonder at,
I come again, to tower and lurch and spill.

Dunvegan

High in the air, the air
Lies like an open secret;
It loosens its fist and lets
Islands float in to where

Round heads bob on the green –
Their dogs' eyes follow the dinghy
Crabbing across the tide.
Two cliffs and a sea between

Have stolen a space of time
And squander it all in being;
The sea thrills like a silence
Between a chime and a chime:

And the rowan digs its claws
Into the heart of the matter
And a rose is Lazarus and
Shuffling ripples are flaws

Through which the mind can see
What way the wind is blowing –
As this one, that drifts in
Over the boulder scree,

Where ducks squatter in mud
And, cubed on a kilted stone,
Stands the grey honeycomb
Filled with claret and blood

Where a great music arose
And Mary, Red Alasdair's daughter,
Made poems and ladled her snuff
Into her randy nose.

Sabbath

The water makes a glittering sound. The bush
It makes it in becomes a bell of light.
Something like laughter marries into space
And fills its gay rooms with a dancing rush.
Time at the door stands with averted face.

Steep down, or up, translucencies conspire
To give themselves away, sheeting themselves
Only with watery othernesses. Hill
Humbles no grassblade and short shadows pour
Their horns of grace and tremble where they spill.

To speak a word or to be spoken by
A nearly word, a word becoming word . . .
Long blood in crimson could not come to this
Nor cross grown heavy in its shroud of gray
Nor silver tarnished with a Judas kiss.

Something flies lightly. Something in the grass
Speaks with a bearded hilarity. Something is
A garden with a tree in it whose fruit
Hangs from a twig, a branch, a bole that digs
Deep in this moment, now, its secret root.

Loch na Bearraig

It makes no claim – as though a claim could be
Colour of islands, absence of a tree
Or cliff on one side sailing to the sea.

And no solution can be made to fit
The clues it gives, however composite
Of ravens above Glen Canisp, deer in it.

If two mergansers, beak to beak, swim round
Their kissing centre, that is what they've found
And flouncing water is their loving sound.

And drifting flies, whose jury sails can do
No more than keep them head to wind, pursue
Their own solution and a different clue.

Even light stays universal – though it has needs
That it expresses, trailing in long screeds
Or sparking epigrams in a bed of weeds.

And trout swim separate in their private cold,
Even if it seems, so closely are they shoaled,
It is their wavering turns the water gold.

It has no claim: is one. Its water makes
For beaches other than those on which it breaks
And its waves die for more than their own sakes.

A true decorum, where an abstraction finds
Easy admittance and haunts these rocky wynds,
Filthy and roaring for its sidling hinds.

John Quixote

Where he jogs dusty, trailing a horn of dust,
Ironic windmills signal through gray air
Their huge tall jokes and a lousy innkeeper
Spreads evil blankets, swansdown to his pelt;
Princes in pigsties scratch their scurfy crust
And heads of heathens stutter at his belt.

No lark so ravishing as to be a lark
Nor dirt so true as nourish one poor seed.
His mad eye twitches, hands grope for a deed
That would free heavenly hosts to sing and soar
Over gold acres, dancing round the Ark.
(He halts at byre-ends, snuffing the devil's spoor).

No fat self follows him to keep him wrong.
High in his proper sun his high casque jogs
By scarps and enfilading gorges, dogs
Snarling in worlds below where wit and grace
And bestial scholars and thin priests belong.
– By tumbling in the dust he proves his case.

His chattering armour squeaks there as he sprawls
Under the laughing bellies, and his lance,
Clenched in his claw still, wavers through mischance
To point, true North, at his old target, till,
His beard cocked high, he clatters off and bawls
Tremendous lovesongs to the tiny hills.

Brackloch

There was a branch
Was in a bush was in a wood was in
What became parcelled in my careless skin.

Colours went by
As shades of colours, and a rose tree was
Where space must thicken and where time must pause.

By a roadside
A water made away with itself and stayed.
Only by it was silence disarrayed.

And silence, by
That sweet dishevelling made lovelier,
Fell silent all the more and would not stir.

The man going by,
As though a mind were an informing grace,
Put on the being of that common place.

He was therefore
Enriched by bank and wall and, there, beyond,
A star being glow-worm on a bracken frond.

And structures rose
Into a future that is now where these
Long buried things are present histories.

Work in Progress

Curl creamy angels on the blue,
With every cloud a puffing boy
And dolphins blowing to the true
North in every corner.

Ships, elegantly wrecked, toss out
Toy mariners, caught as they sprawl,
As though all threaded down the snout
Of an old gin bottle.

A few crimped waves will frill the foot
Of paradisal reefs whereon
Brown seabeasts scurf their scales and flute
A minuet of Mozart.

And now a mermaid, fancy-free,
Blank-eyed and draggle-tailed in surf –
Erotic image that the sea
Has not a thing to do with.

The whole thing's framed. The artist, faint
With visionary exertions, knows
A storm howls underneath the paint
And wrecks rot under canvas.

And now, a pastoral, perhaps? –
With haywains carting judgments home
And lowing cows (God's thunderclaps)
And pert milkmaids (the Furies).

Romantic Sunset

The purple flare made images, of course,
In the image-mad; and was a purple flare
Of one huge pulse upon the darkening air.

Proximity, too, rolled up its sleeves and took
From nothing there engaging miracles
To make sand not sand and hills sudden hills.

Even a mind, made numinous of itself,
Achieved the image of being an actual fact;
Aesthetics painting what its substance lacked.

And gods, of kinds, and meanings, of a sort,
Emerged from a worn seascape and became
Its substitute, and seemed the very same.

A revelation, murmured the mad mind,
Expanding through affinities till it was
So near divine it was almost its own Cause.

And contemplations of pure being breathed
Serenity and grace where, overhead,
Blue seduced green and purple savaged red.

Explorer

Trampling new seas with filthy timbers, he
Jotted down headlands, speculated on
Vestigial civilisations, ate strange fruits
And called his officers Mister. When sails were gone

Bundling and tumbling down the shrieking dark,
He trailed the Bible as sea-anchor; when
Reefs shaved the barnacles from the keel, he took
His gentlemanly snuff. Each night at ten,

Under the lamp from which his cabin swung,
He logged the latest, drank his grog and spread,
With only one uncomprehending sigh,
His wild uncharted world upon his bed.

July Evening

A bird's voice chinks and tinkles
Alone in the gaunt reedbed –
    Tiny silversmith
Working late in the evening.

I sit and listen. The rooftop
With a quill of smoke stuck in it
    Wavers against the sky
In the dreamy heat of summer.

Flowers' closing time: bee lurches
Across the hayfield, singing
    And feeling its drunken way
Round the air's invisible corners.

And grass is grace. And charlock
Is gold of its own bounty.
    The broken chair by the wall
Is all of immortal landscapes.

Something has been completed
That everything is part of,
    Something that will go on
Being completed forever.

Upper Circle

The notes swirled outwards in a buzzing swarm.
The silence, stirred, was whirlpools, each a flower
The notes died into, vanishing from harm.
(Clouds melt in sight some days and breed again
Before they die and murder their young rain).

Having disordered what awaited them,
The notes died, too, but left an order there,
As though dropped petals froze back on their stem –
A ghost bush fading in substance of the air:
The flowers go first, leaving the branches bare.

Some sort of sacrifice had taken place,
A ritual murder of an ugly thing
Or god, or both, whose resurrected face
Gave his death meaning; and his rising was
Grace hammered out and formalised as laws.

Outside, the street swirled, swarming in a night
That waited to be understood. Cars drove
Into their silences. – What meaning might
Be walking there, a lonely Christ, disguised
As his true self and so unrecognised?

A Good Day

Sun-stunned the water; trees hold their breath.
The bracken smell is six foot deep
And never stirs. I feel green crumbs of heather
Crawling on cheekbones . . . Stillness but not sleep.

A heron, folded round himself,
Stands in the ebb, as I in mine.
I feel my world beneath me, like his, shelving
To darker depths of dark and bitter brine.

Suddenly round the cliff face bolt
Pigeon and falcon – they tear the air
And are gone in it. And the day stands, without motion,
As though nothing had drawn that savage blue stroke there.

What has been wounded? Only false
Images. Nothing can betray
Wise heron, shattering light or breathless alder
Or water slipping soundlessly away.

Old Man

The moonstreak shone green-gilded through the room,
Apprentice ghost, no proper revenant,
But matchlessly aloof; and softly, boom!

And softly, boom! the waves crushed on the sand
And night spread its immaculate distances.
He sat in darkness and his heavy hand

Lay clenched in other times. His face was stone
Or timber, rather, rejected by long tides:
Experience, not feeling. Hills of bone

And small pragmatic ships and curving shores
Loosened the mind they were composed of through
Weddings and storms and nettle-foundered doors

And into blazing immaculate distances.
How a carved eyelid shuts no sunlight out
Or knotted tongue finds nothing to dispraise

Or hand fails to unclench and reject it all –
Till the green moonstreak lipped his foot and he
Scraped the chair sideways, closer to the wall.

After Rain

A dead fish rotted in the air –
A cloud it was, really; and small
Waterclocks ticked and faded, smaller
And fewer, in the bushes, where
Stems shone like tubes of coloured water.

Roads panted upward and on crests
Trembled out into space. What true
Limit divides two sorts of blueness?
Or takes one man from all the rest?
Or calls this wood and calls that forest?

The sun unclenched a cloud and made
Small puddles slowly close their eyes.
– Water fell upwards and its rising
Through such an intercourse of shades
Was light, or light with water married.

False limits spiralled everywhere
Round stone, leaf, light, bush, water, cloud
And bound them all in one. They foundered
From their own selves, as ghosts in air,
Or thought in words, or light in water.

The cloud, that ghost fish in the sky,
Unpicked itself into the blue;
And any thought dissolved in truer
Forms, whose wavering boundary
Was thought when thought and feeling marry.

And time that ticked more slowly in
The drying bushes still was one
Mode of itself that stills a thunder,
Teaches a wave when to begin
And kills a year with one last minute.

100240

Purification

Winds whirl in their hooded caves
And tawny rocks are all asleep.
Easy to see the moon walk on this desert,
Easy to see her, smiling to herself.

Yesterday winds howled overhead,
Lions loped in the cruel light,
Cities crawled in the glare, and the horizon
Flickered with journeys, dreams, abandonments.

Wearing your self as though it were
The lightest of all garments, moving
As though all answers were a mode of movement,
You came and were as though to be were easy.

And now there is an end of storm,
Of rage and lust and wild horizons.
Desert is purely desert, in itself . . .
To be a desert, even, is difficult.

Thaw on a Building Site

The strong sun changed the air; drops
Trembled down, expired upwards.
Saucer crusts of earth collapsed.
Extraordinary pools appeared.

And reddish planks turned yellow;
A concrete mixer cleared its throat
For a boring speech, all consonants. Slow
Troglodytes came from the hut.

They swarmed in air, on earth, beneath it,
Crept in and out of space, informed
It with a ghost of shape – breathing
Not yet a language, but its grammar.

Wheelbarrows shot up thirty feet.
A ripped plank screamed. And, slowly, buildings
Backed their way into the light;
They crumbled upwards into being.

Dinghy Skirting a Reef

Ploughshare that leaves no furrow
Slides through the crumbling water
Where tigerish mackerel go
Slashing through shoals of fry –
The seething brine is bitter
But not because they die.

A cormorant, unfrocked priest
Gross on the groaning skerry,
Parodies holy Easter.
He hangs on the cosy Cross
Of his own skeleton there,
Gorged on his natural Logos.

Up feathers a naked figure,
Pauses, collapses, shot
In the hollow breast by a rainbow
And, pattering sideways, rests
In his Abraham's bosom of water,
His lecherous old ancestor.

The brown sail wags, leans over
And the whole world spins round
The solid brain at the centre –
Blobbed in the middlemost middle
Of a web of grace abounding,
At once shrill fly, cold spider.

Ambiguous Snow

Snowfalls make no insinuations.
Silence in a white disguise
Happens, without rhetoric
Of slamming clouds and slipshod raindrops.

Posts are mushroomed, roofs are frilled;
Light bangs on the sparkling snow-crust;
Thin wires balance mountain ranges;
Branches break off at the wrist.

Pretty ambiguity, where
Great stags smother, armies founder
In a mad pastry-cook's mad vision,
Pretty in the Christmas candles.

And the word creeps through the snow,
Black as pavements, green as crocus;
And the snuggling bud is warm;
And the thrush dies in his feathers.

Canal in Winter

The wind makes flags of posters;
Small grins of bubbles break
Uneasily on the thick
Scum matted on green water.

Slowly a rotting warehouse
Steps down another inch
Into the mud, from which
Weeds float on dying journeys.

The towpath creaks with wintry
Cat-ice; pincushion grass
Is frosted on walls where slime
Draws maps of every country.

Doom and decay, inflicting
Their beauty here, disclose
Themselves as vocables:
A human mind's reflection.

The other facts care nothing;
They ease a landscape towards
New forms, through filth and mud
Where a new life is seething.

And the corrupt reed, leaning
Over its own downfall,
Sets out on a never final
Stage of its endless journey.

DATE DUE